BIBLE
PROMISES
for
MEN

PUBLISHING GROUP

NASHVILLE, TENNESSEE

Bible Promises for Men
Copyright © 2003 by B&H Publishing Group
Updated and Reprinted, 2008
All Rights Reserved

ISBN: 978-0-8054-4767-5
B&H Publishing Group
Nashville, Tennessee
www.BHPublishingGroup.com

All Scripture verses are taken from the Holman
Christian Standard Bible®, Copyright © 1999,
2000, 2002, 2003 by Holman Bible Publishers.

Dewey Decimal Classification: 242.643
Men / God—Promises / Devotional Literature

Printed in the United States of America
5 6 7 8 9   17 16 15 14 13

TABLE *of* CONTENTS

PROMISES
for
EVERYDAY LIFE

When we confine the Bible to the formality of Sunday mornings, we miss the daily essence of the Scripture—the ability of God's truth to travel along with us into staff meetings or onto the assembly line, to remain with us while we're pulling weeds in the vegetable garden or clearing snow from the front walk.

God's Word has been given to us not only to inspire us in expected settings, but also to infuse God's presence into places where we could easily ignore him—but where we need Him every hour, every minute, every day.

DEALING
with
STRESS

I Don't Know If I Can Take Much More

God is our refuge and strength,
    a helper who is always found
    in times of trouble.
Therefore we will not be afraid,
    though the earth trembles
    and the mountains topple
    into the depths of the seas,
    though its waters roar and foam
    and the mountains quake with its turmoil.
      —Psalm 46:1–3

Trouble and distress terrify him, overwhelming
him like a king prepared for battle.
—*Job 15:24*

Show us favor, Lord, show us favor,
    for we've had more than enough contempt.
—*Psalm 123:3*

God, hear my cry;
    pay attention to my prayer.
I call to You from the ends of the earth
    when my heart is without strength.
Lead me to a rock that is high above me,
    for You have been a refuge for me,
    a strong tower in the face of the enemy.
I will live in Your tent forever
    and take refuge
    under the shelter of Your wings. . . .
Then I will continually sing of Your name,
    fulfilling my vows day by day.
—*Psalm 61:1–4, 8*

This is the day the Lord has made;
    let us rejoice and be glad in it.
Lord, save us! Lord, please grant us success!
—*Psalm 118:24–25*

I exclaimed, "This is my intense suffering,
but I must bear it."
—*Jeremiah 10:19b*

For consider Him who endured such
hostility from sinners against Himself, so
that you won't grow weary and lose heart.
—*Hebrews 12:3*

Stop your fighting—and know that I am God,
exalted among the nations,
exalted on the earth.
—*Psalm 46:10*

He saw them being battered as they rowed,
because the wind was against them.

Around three in the morning He came
toward them walking on the sea and wanted to
pass by them. When they saw Him walking on
the sea, they thought it was a ghost and cried
out; for they all saw Him and were terrified.

Immediately He spoke with them and said,
"Have courage! It is I. Don't be afraid." Then
He got into the boat with them, and the wind
ceased.
—*Mark 6:48–51*

Peace I leave with you. My peace I give to you. I do not give to you as the world gives. Your heart must not be troubled or fearful.
—*John 14:27*

For the waywardness
of the inexperienced will kill them,
and the complacency of fools
will destroy them.
But whoever listens to me will live securely
and be free from the fear of danger.
—*Proverbs 1:32–33*

The Bible is the one book to which any thoughtful man may go with any honest question of life or destiny and find the answer of God by honest searching.
—*John Ruskin*

For as the sufferings of Christ overflow to us, so our comfort overflows through Christ. If we are afflicted, it is for your comfort and salvation; if we are comforted, it is for your comfort, which is experienced in the endurance of the same sufferings that we suffer. . . .

For we don't want you to be unaware, brothers, of our affliction that took place in the province of Asia: we were completely overwhelmed—beyond our strength—so that we even despaired of life. However, we personally had a death sentence within ourselves so that we would not trust in ourselves, but in God who raises the dead.

He has delivered us from such a terrible death, and He will deliver us; we have placed our hope in Him that He will deliver us again.
—*2 Corinthians 1:5–6, 8–10*

Therefore don't worry about tomorrow, because tomorrow will worry about itself. Each day has enough trouble of its own.
—*Matthew 6:34*

But as for you, keep a clear head about everything, endure hardship, do the work of an evangelist, fulfill your ministry.
—*2 Timothy 4:5*

Share in suffering as a good soldier of Christ.
—*2 Timothy 2:3*

Strengthen your tired hands and weakened knees, and make straight paths for your feet, so that what is lame may not be dislocated, but healed instead.
—*Hebrews 12:12–13*

Say to the faint-hearted:
"Be strong; do not fear!"
—*Isaiah 35:4a*

DESIRING DISCIPLINE

I Need to Finish What I've Started

For this very reason, make every effort to supplement your faith with goodness, goodness with knowledge, knowledge with self-control, self-control with endurance, endurance with godliness, godliness with brotherly affection, and brotherly affection with love. For if these qualities are yours and are increasing, they will keep you from being useless or unfruitful in the knowledge of our Lord Jesus Christ.
—*2 Peter 1:5–8*

Patience is better than power,
    and controlling one's temper,
    than capturing a city.
    —*Proverbs 16:32*

For when we were in the flesh, the sinful passions operated through the law in every part of us and bore fruit for death.

But now we have been released from the law, since we have died to what held us, so that we may serve in the new way of the Spirit and not in the old letter of the law.
    —*Romans 7:5–6*

Therefore, get your minds ready for action, being self-disciplined, and set your hope completely on the grace to be brought to you at the revelation of Jesus Christ.

As obedient children, do not be conformed to the desires of your former ignorance but, as the One who called you is holy, you also are to be holy in all your conduct; for it is written, Be holy, because I am holy.
    —*1 Peter 1:13–16*

LORD, You are our Father;
　　we are the clay, and You are our potter;
　　we all are the work of Your hands.
　　　　—Isaiah 64:8

Christ has liberated us into freedom.
　　Therefore stand firm and don't
　　submit again to a yoke of slavery.
　　　　—Galatians 6:1

I will instruct you and show you the way to go;
　　with My eye on you, I will give counsel.
Do not be like a horse or mule,
　　without understanding,
that must be controlled with bit and bridle,
　　or else it will not come near you.
Many pains come to the wicked,
　　but the one who trusts in the LORD
　　will have faithful love surrounding him.
　　　　—Psalm 32:8–10

I love those who love me,
　　and those who search for me find me.
　　　　—Proverbs 8:17

So then, brothers, we are not obligated to the flesh to live according to the flesh, for if you live according to the flesh, you are going to die. But if by the Spirit you put to death the deeds of the body, you will live.

—*Romans 8:12–13*

But endurance must do its complete work, so that you may be mature and complete, lacking nothing.

—*James 1:4*

Scholars may quote Plato in their studies, but the hearts of millions will quote the Bible at their daily toil, and draw strength from its inspiration, as the meadows draw it from the brook.

—*M. Daniel Conway*

Endure it as discipline: God is dealing with you as sons. For what son is there whom a father does not discipline? But if you are without discipline—which all receive—then you are illegitimate children and not sons.

Furthermore, we had natural fathers discipline us, and we respected them. Shouldn't we submit even more to the Father of spirits and live? For they disciplined us for a short time based on what seemed good to them, but He does it for our benefit, so that we can share His holiness.

No discipline seems enjoyable at the time, but painful. Later on, however, it yields the fruit of peace and righteousness to those who have been trained by it.

—*Hebrews 12:7–11*

If anyone wants to come with Me, he must deny himself, take up his cross daily, and follow Me. For whoever wants to save his life will lose it, but whoever loses his life because of Me will save it. What is a man benefited if he gains the whole world, yet loses or forfeits himself?

—*Luke 9:23–25*

But the fruit of the Spirit is love, joy, peace, patience, kindness, goodness, faith, gentleness, self-control. Against such things there is no law.

Now those who belong to Christ Jesus have crucified the flesh with its passions and desires. If we live by the Spirit, we must also follow the Spirit.

—*Galatians 5:22–25*

Be sober! Be on the alert! Your adversary the Devil is prowling around like a roaring lion, looking for anyone he can devour.

Resist him, firm in the faith, knowing that the same sufferings are being experienced by your brothers in the world.

—*1 Peter 5:8–9*

SHOOTING
for
BALANCE

Am I All Work and No Play?

Remember to dedicate the Sabbath day: You are to labor six days and do all your work, but the seventh day is a Sabbath to the LORD your God. . . . For the LORD made the heavens and the earth, the sea, and everything in them in six days; then He rested on the seventh day. Therefore the LORD blessed the Sabbath day and declared it holy.
—*Exodus 20:8–10a, 11*

Do not lack diligence; be fervent in spirit; serve the Lord.
—*Romans 12:11*

Now we command and exhort such people, by the Lord Jesus Christ, that quietly working, they may eat their own bread. Brothers, do not grow weary in doing good.
—*2 Thessalonians 3:12–13*

But we encourage you, brothers, to do so even more, to seek to lead a quiet life, to mind your own business, and to work with your own hands, as we commanded you, so that you may walk properly in the presence of outsiders and not be dependent on anyone.
—*1 Thessalonians 4:10b–12*

And whatever you do, in word or in deed, do everything in the name of the Lord Jesus, giving thanks to God the Father through Him.
—*Colossians 3:17*

What does the worker gain from his struggles? I have seen the task that God has given people to keep them occupied. He has made everything appropriate in its time. He has also put eternity in their hearts, but man cannot discover the work God has done from beginning to end.

I know that there is nothing better for them than to rejoice and enjoy the good life. It is also the gift of God whenever anyone eats, drinks, and enjoys all his efforts.

—*Ecclesiastes 3:9–13*

Therefore, whether you eat or drink, or whatever you do, do everything for God's glory.

—*1 Corinthians 10:31*

You are to conduct yourselves in reverence during this time of temporary residence. For you know that you were redeemed from your empty way of life inherited from the fathers, not with perishable things, like silver or gold, but with the precious blood of Christ.

—*1 Peter 1:17b–19a*

Now the end of all things is near; therefore, be clear-headed and disciplined for prayer. . . . Based on the gift they have received, everyone should use it to serve others, as good managers of the varied grace of God.

If anyone speaks, his speech should be like the oracles of God; if anyone serves, his service should be from the strength God provides, so that in everything God may be glorified through Jesus Christ. To Him belong the glory and the power forever and ever. Amen.

—*1 Peter 4:7, 10–11*

The Bible goes equally to the cottage of the peasant and the palace of the king. It enters men's closets, directs their conduct, and mingles in all the grief and cheerfulness of life.

—*Theodore Parker*

There is an occasion for everything,
and a time for every activity under heaven:
a time to give birth and a time to die;
a time to plant and a time to uproot;
a time to kill and a time to heal;
a time to tear down and a time to build;
a time to weep and a time to laugh;
a time to mourn and a time to dance;
a time to throw stones
and a time to gather stones;
a time to embrace
and a time to avoid embracing;
a time to search and a time to count as lost;
a time to keep and a time to throw away;
a time to tear and a time to sew;
a time to be silent and a time to speak;
a time to love and a time to hate;
a time for war and a time for peace.
—*Ecclesiastes 3:1–8*

Be in agreement with one another. Do not be proud; instead, associate with the humble. Do not be wise in your own estimation. Do not repay anyone evil for evil. Try to do what is honorable in everyone's eyes. If possible, on your part, live at peace with everyone.

—*Romans 12:16–18*

For if anyone considers himself to be something when he is nothing, he is deceiving himself. But each person should examine his own work, and then he will have a reason for boasting in himself alone, and not in respect to someone else. For each person will have to carry his own load.

—*Galatians 6:3–5*

If anyone thinks he is religious, without controlling his tongue but deceiving his heart, his religion is useless. Pure and undefiled religion before our God and Father is this: to look after orphans and widows in their distress and to keep oneself unstained by the world.

—*James 1:26–27*

Making Good Decisions

Sometimes I Just Don't Know What to Do

Now if any of you lacks wisdom, he should ask God, who gives to all generously and without criticizing, and it will be given to him.

But let him ask in faith without doubting. For the doubter is like the surging sea, driven and tossed by the wind. That person should not expect to receive anything from the Lord. An indecisive man is unstable in all his ways.

—James 1:5–8

Brothers, don't be childish in your
thinking, but be infants in evil and adult
in your thinking.
    —*1 Corinthians 14:20*

Trust in the LORD with all your heart,
    and do not rely
    on your own understanding;
think about Him in all your ways,
    and He will guide you on the right paths.
Don't consider yourself to be wise;
    fear the LORD and turn away from evil.
    —*Proverbs 3:5–7*

Pay careful attention, then, to how you
walk—not as unwise people but as wise—
making the most of the time, because the days
are evil. So don't be foolish, but understand
what the Lord's will is.
    —*Ephesians 5:15-17*

Do not be conformed to this age, but be
transformed by the renewing of your mind,
so that you may discern what is the good,
pleasing, and perfect will of God.
    —*Romans 12:2*

You teach me wisdom deep within.
—*Psalm 51:6*

But be doers of the word and not hearers
only, deceiving yourselves. Because if anyone is
a hearer of the word and not a doer, he is like
a man looking at his own face in a mirror; for
he looks at himself, goes away, and right away
forgets what kind of man he was.

But the one who looks intently into the
perfect law of freedom and perseveres in it, and
is not a forgetful hearer but a doer who acts—
this person will be blessed in what he does.
—*James 1:22–25*

The Spirit of the LORD will rest on Him—
    a Spirit of wisdom and understanding,
    a Spirit of counsel and strength,
    a Spirit of knowledge
    and of the fear of the LORD.
       —*Isaiah 11:2*

Then you will understand
    righteousness, justice,
    and integrity—every good path.
       —*Proverbs 2:9*

For wisdom will enter your mind,
and knowledge will delight your heart.
Discretion will watch over you,
and understanding will guard you,
—Proverbs 2:10–11

Wisdom is better than weapons of war.
—Ecclesiastes 9:18a

The real influence of the Bible cannot be measured. It is reckoned only in terms of hearts that have been lifted up, decisions that have been changed, men and women who, in response to its impervious demands, have done justice and loved kindness and walked humbly with their God.
—J. Carter Swain

My son, if you accept my words
    and store up my commands within you,
listening closely to wisdom
    and directing your heart to understanding;
furthermore, if you call out to insight
    and lift your voice to understanding,
if you seek it like silver
    and search for it like hidden treasure,
then you will understand the fear of the LORD
    and discover the knowledge of God.
For the LORD gives wisdom;
    from His mouth come
    knowledge and understanding.
He stores up success for the upright;
    He is a shield for those
    who live with integrity
so that He may guard the paths of justice
    and protect the way of His loyal followers.
       —Proverbs 2:1–8

Now everyone who lives on milk is inexperienced with the message about righteousness, because he is an infant. But solid food is for the mature—for those whose senses have been trained to distinguish between good and evil.
—*Hebrews 5:13–14*

This also comes from the LORD of Hosts.
He gives wonderful advice;
He gives great wisdom.
—*Isaiah 28:29*

He gives wisdom to the wise
and knowledge to those
who have understanding.
He reveals the deep and hidden things;
He knows what is in the darkness,
and light dwells with Him.
I offer thanks and praise to You,
God of my fathers,
because You have given me
wisdom and power.
And now You have let me know
what we asked of You.
—*Daniel 2:21b–23a*

Mastering
Your
Money

How Well Am I Handling My Finances?

Instruct those who are rich in the present age not to be arrogant or to set their hope on the uncertainty of wealth, but on God, who richly provides us with all things to enjoy.

Instruct them to do good, to be rich in good works, to be generous, willing to share, storing up for themselves a good foundation for the age to come, so that they may take hold of life that is real.

—*1 Timothy 6:17–19*

The one who loves money is never satisfied with money, and whoever loves wealth is never satisfied with income.
—*Ecclesiastes 5:10a*

For we brought nothing into the world, and we can take nothing out. But if we have food and clothing, we will be content with these.

But those who want to be rich fall into temptation, a trap, and many foolish and harmful desires, which plunge people into ruin and destruction. For the love of money is a root of all kinds of evil, and by craving it, some have wandered away from the faith and pierced themselves with many pains.
—*1 Timothy 6:7–10*

Your life should be free from the love of money. Be satisfied with what you have.
—*Hebrews 13:5a*

A faithful man will have many blessings.
—*Proverbs 28:20a*

Honor the LORD with your possessions
  and with the first produce
  of your entire harvest;
then your barns will be completely filled,
  and your vats will overflow with new wine.
    —*Proverbs 3:9–10*

"Bring the full 10 percent into the storehouse so that there may be food in My house. Test Me in this way," says the LORD of Hosts. "See if I will not open the floodgates of heaven and pour out a blessing for you without measure. I will rebuke the devourer for you, so that it will not ruin the produce of your ground, and your vine in your field will not be barren," says the LORD of Hosts. "Then all the nations will consider you fortunate, for you will be a delightful land," says the LORD of Hosts.
    —*Malachi 3:10–12*

Give, and it will be given to you; a good measure—pressed down, shaken together, and running over—will be poured into your lap. For with the measure you use, it will be measured back to you.
    —*Luke 6:38*

Remember this: the person who sows sparingly will also reap sparingly, and the person who sows generously will also reap generously. Each person should do as he has decided in his heart—not out of regret or out of necessity, for God loves a cheerful giver. And God is able to make every grace overflow to you, so that in every way, always having everything you need, you may excel in every good work.

—*2 Corinthians 9:6–8*

Most people are bothered by the passages in Scripture which they cannot understand; but as for me, I always noticed that the passages in Scripture which trouble me most are those which I do understand.

—*Mark Twain*

Don't collect for yourselves treasures on earth, where moth and rust destroy and where thieves break in and steal.

But collect for yourselves treasures in heaven, where neither moth nor rust destroys, and where thieves don't break in and steal. For where your treasure is, there your heart will be also.

The eye is the lamp of the body. If your eye is good, your whole body will be full of light. But if your eye is bad, your whole body will be full of darkness. So if the light within you is darkness—how deep is that darkness!

No one can be a slave of two masters, since either he will hate one and love the other, or be devoted to one and despise the other. You cannot be slaves of God and of money.

—*Matthew 6:19–24*

Pay your obligations to everyone: taxes
to those you owe taxes, tolls to those you owe
tolls, respect to those you owe respect, and
honor to those you owe honor.
—*Romans 13:7*

Better a poor man who lives with integrity
    than a rich man who
    distorts right and wrong.
    —*Proverbs 28:6*

Why does a fool have money in his hand
    with no intention of buying wisdom?
    —*Proverbs 17:16*

A good name is to be chosen over great wealth;
    favor is better than silver and gold.
    —*Proverbs 22:1*

Don't work for the food that perishes but
for the food that lasts for eternal life, which
the Son of Man will give you, because God the
Father has set His seal of approval on Him.
    —*John 6:27*

PROMISES
for
YOUR
FAMILY

If you're a husband or father, your duties and responsibilities run a lot deeper than repairing leaky faucets and changing light bulbs. People's lives are depending on your leadership, in need of your discretion and judgment, weakened without your prayers.

So the Bible is your guidebook to what love looks like in the eyes and actions of a husband, what compassion feels like around the shoulders of a child, or what it means to give back to your own parents for their love toward you. You are a man charged with people's futures, and you need God's help to do it well.

THE GIFT
of
CHILDREN

I Hope They Know How Much I Love Them

Sons are indeed a heritage from the LORD,
   children, a reward.
Like arrows in the hand of a warrior
   are the sons born in one's youth.
Happy is the man who has filled his quiver
with them.
      Such men will never be put to shame
      when they speak with their enemies
      at the city gate.
         —*Psalm 127:3–5*

Come, children, listen to me;
    I will teach you the fear of the LORD.
Who is the man who delights in life,
    loving a long life to enjoy what is good?
Keep your tongue from evil
    and your lips from deceitful speech.
Turn away from evil and do what is good;
        seek peace and pursue it.
            —*Psalm 34:11–14*

In the fear of the LORD
        one has strong confidence
        and his children have a refuge.
            —*Proverbs 14:26*

He protects His flock like a shepherd;
        He gathers the lambs in His arms
and carries them in the fold
        of His garment.
            —*Isaiah 40:11a*

For I have chosen him so that he will
command his children and his house after
him to keep the way of the LORD by doing
what is right and just.
            —*Genesis 18:19a*

Discipline your son,
    and he will give you comfort;
    he will also give you delight.
        —*Proverbs 29:17*

Do not despise the Lord's instruction, my son,
    and do not loathe His discipline;
for the Lord disciplines the one He loves,
    just as a father, the son he delights in.
        —*Proverbs 3:11–12*

What man among you, if his son asks him
for bread, will give him a stone? Or if he asks
for a fish, will give him a snake?
    If you then, who are evil, know how to give
good gifts to your children, how much more
will your Father in heaven give good things to
those who ask Him!
        —*Matthew 7:9–11*

Fathers, don't stir up anger in your children, but bring them up in the training and
instruction of the Lord.
        —*Ephesians 6:4*

The one who will not use the rod
    hates his son,
but the one who loves him
    disciplines him diligently.
       —*Proverbs 13:24*

There are thorns and snares
    on the path of the crooked;
the one who guards himself
    stays far from them.
Teach a youth about the way he should go;
    even when he is old
    he will not depart from it.
       —*Proverbs 22:5–6*

If there is anything in my thoughts or style
to commend, the credit is due to my parents
for instilling in me an early love of the Scriptures. If we abide by the principles taught
there, our country will go on prospering.
       —*Daniel Webster*

My people, hear my instruction;
    listen to what I say.
I will declare wise sayings;
    I will speak mysteries from the past—
things we have heard and known
    and that our fathers
    have passed down to us.
We must not hide them from their children,
    but must tell a future generation
the praises of the LORD,
    His might, and the wonderful works
    He has performed.
He established a testimony in Jacob
    and set up a law in Israel,
which He commanded our fathers
    to teach to their children
so that a future generation—
    children yet to be born—might know.
They were to rise and tell their children
    so that they might
    put their confidence in God
and not forget God's works,
    but keep His commandments.
        —*Psalm 78:1–7*

See that you don't look down on one
of these little ones, because I tell you that in
heaven their angels continually view the face
of My Father in heaven. . . .

What do you think? If a man has 100
sheep, and one of them goes astray, won't he
leave the 99 on the hillside and go and search
for the stray? And if he finds it, I assure you:
He rejoices over that sheep more than over the
99 that did not go astray. In the same way, it is
not the will of your Father in heaven that one
of these little ones perish.

—*Matthew 18:10, 12–14*

Whoever welcomes one little child such as
this in My name welcomes Me.

—*Mark 9:37a*

I am not seeking what is yours, but you.
For children are not obligated to save up for
their parents, but parents for their children. I
will most gladly spend and be spent for you.

—*2 Corinthians 12:14b–15a*

THE
COVENANT
of
MARRIAGE

When You Gave Me a Wife,
You Gave Me a Friend

The man said: "This one, at last, is bone of my bone, and flesh of my flesh; this one will be called woman, for she was taken from man."

This is why a man leaves his father and mother and bonds with his wife, and they become one flesh.

—*Genesis 2:23–24*

Husbands, love your wives, just as also Christ loved the church and gave Himself for her, to make her holy, cleansing her in the washing of water by the word.

He did this to present the church to Himself in splendor, without spot or wrinkle or any such thing, but holy and blameless.
—Ephesians 5:25–27

Husbands, in the same way, live with your wives with understanding of their weaker nature yet showing them honor as co-heirs of the grace of life, so that your prayers will not be hindered.
—1 Peter 3:7

With all humility and gentleness, with patience, accepting one another in love.
—Ephesians 4:2

A man who finds a wife finds a good thing and obtains favor from the LORD.
—Proverbs 18:22

A husband should fulfill his marital duty to his wife, and likewise a wife to her husband.

A wife does not have authority over her own body, but her husband does. Equally, a husband does not have authority over his own body, but his wife does.

—*1 Corinthians 7:3–4*

I have made a covenant with my eyes.
    How then could I look at a young woman?
For what portion would
    I have from God above,
or what inheritance
    from the Almighty on high?
Doesn't disaster come to the wicked
    and misfortune to evildoers?
Does He not see my ways
    and number all my steps?
        —*Job 31:1–4*

Marriage must be respected by all, and the marriage bed kept undefiled.
        —*Hebrews 13:4a*

Drink water from your own cistern,
    water flowing from your own well.
Should your springs flow in the streets,
    streams of water in the public squares?
They should be for you alone
    and not for you to share with strangers.
Let your fountain be blessed,
    and take pleasure
    in the wife of your youth.
A loving doe, a graceful fawn—
    let her breasts always satisfy you;
    be lost in her love forever.
      —Proverbs 5:15–19

    The Word of Scripture should never stop sounding in your ears and working in you all day long, just like the words of someone you love.

    —Dietrich Bonhoeffer

Wives, submit to your own husbands as to the Lord, for the husband is head of the wife as also Christ is head of the church. He is the Savior of the body. . . .

In the same way, husbands should love their wives as their own bodies. He who loves his wife loves himself. For no one ever hates his own flesh, but provides and cares for it, just as Christ does for the church, since we are members of His body.

"For this reason a man will leave his father and mother and be joined to his wife, and the two will become one flesh." This mystery is profound, but I am talking about Christ and the church.

To sum up, each one of you is to love his wife as himself, and the wife is to respect her husband.

—Ephesians 5:22–23, 28–33

How beautiful you are, my darling.
   How very beautiful!
   Your eyes are doves.
      —*Song of Songs 1:15*

Like a lily among thorns,
   so is my darling among the young women.
      —*Song of Songs 2:2*

Love's flames are fiery flames—
   the fiercest of all.
Mighty waters cannot extinguish love;
   rivers cannot sweep it away.
      —*Song of Songs 8:6b–7a*

Arise, my darling.
   Come away, my beautiful one.
      —*Song of Songs 2:13b*

You have captured my heart
   with one glance of your eyes.
      —*Song of Songs 4:9b*

THE NEED
for
LEADERSHIP

I Want to Be Strong for My Family

I will lead the blind
    by a way they did not know;
I will guide them on paths
    they have not known.
I will turn darkness to light in front of them,
    and rough places into level ground.
This is what I will do for them,
    and I will not forsake them.
        —Isaiah 42:16

I thought that age should speak
    and maturity should teach wisdom.
But it is a spirit in man
    and the breath of the Almighty
    that give him understanding.
It is not only the old who are wise or the
    elderly who understand how to judge.
Therefore I say, "Listen to me.
    I too will declare what I know."
        —Job 32:7–10

When He established a limit for the rain
    and a path for the lightning,
He considered wisdom and evaluated it;
    He established it and examined it.
He said to mankind,
    "Look! The fear of the Lord—
that is wisdom, and to turn
    from evil is understanding."
        —Job 28:26–28

When pride comes, disgrace follows,
    but with humility comes wisdom.
The integrity of the upright guides them,
    but the perversity of the
    treacherous destroys them.
        —Proverbs 11:2–3

I pray that the God of our Lord Jesus Christ, the glorious Father, would give you a spirit of wisdom and revelation in the knowledge of Him.

I pray that the eyes of your heart may be enlightened so you may know what is the hope of His calling, what are the glorious riches of His inheritance among the saints, and what is the immeasurable greatness of His power to us who believe, according to the working of His vast strength.

—Ephesians 1:17–19

When the Spirit of truth comes, He will guide you into all the truth. For He will not speak on His own, but He will speak whatever He hears. He will also declare to you what is to come. He will glorify Me, because He will take from what is Mine and declare it to you.

—John 16:13–14

Now we have not received the spirit of the world, but the Spirit who is from God, in order to know what has been freely given to us by God.

—1 Corinthians 2:12

Send Your light and Your truth;
  let them lead me.
Let them bring me to Your holy mountain,
  to Your dwelling place.
  —*Psalm 43:3*

Don't those who plan evil go astray?
  But those who plan good
  find loyalty and faithfulness.
  —*Proverbs 14:22*

A man's heart plans his way,
  but the LORD determines his steps.
  —*Proverbs 16:9*

The man of one book is formidable; but
when that book is the Bible, he is irresistible.
  —*William M. Taylor*

If you get rid of the yoke
    from those around you,
    the finger-pointing and malicious speaking,
and if you offer yourself to the hungry,
    and satisfy the afflicted one,
then your light will shine in the darkness,
    and your night will be like noonday.
The LORD will always lead you,
    satisfy you in a parched land,
    and strengthen your bones.
You will be like a watered garden
    and like a spring
    whose waters never run dry.
Some of you will rebuild the ancient ruins;
    you will restore
    the foundations laid long ago;
you will be called the repairer of broken walls,
    the restorer of streets where people live.
        —Isaiah 58:9b–12

An overseer, therefore, must be above reproach, the husband of one wife, self-controlled, sensible, respectable, hospitable, an able teacher, not addicted to wine, not a bully but gentle, not quarrelsome, not greedy—one who manages his own household competently, having his children under control with all dignity.

—*1 Timothy 3:2–4*

Holding to the faithful message as taught, so that he will be able both to encourage with sound teaching and to refute those who contradict it.

—*Titus 1:9*

The gate is wide and the road is broad that leads to destruction, and there are many who go through it. How narrow is the gate and difficult the road that leads to life, and few find it.

—*Matthew 7:13b–14*

I labor for this, striving with His strength that works powerfully in me.

—*Colossians 1:29*

THE
PURSUIT
of
LEGACY

May I Be Known for Knowing You

But from eternity to eternity
    the LORD's faithful love
    is toward those who fear Him,
and His righteousness toward
    the grandchildren of those
who keep His covenant,
    who remember to observe His instructions.
        —*Psalm 103:17–18*

A good man leaves
   an inheritance to his grandchildren,
but the sinner's wealth
   is stored up for the righteous.
      —*Proverbs 13:22*

The one who lives
   with integrity is righteous;
his children who come
   after him will be happy.
      —*Proverbs 20:7*

   Only be on your guard and diligently
watch yourselves, so that you don't forget the
things your eyes have seen and so that they
don't slip from your mind as long as you live.
Teach them to your children and your
grandchildren.
      —*Deuteronomy 4:9*

   Therefore, be imitators of God, as dearly
loved children.
      —*Ephesians 5:1*

I pray that you, being rooted and firmly established in love, may be able to comprehend with all the saints what is the breadth and width, height and depth, and to know the Messiah's love that surpasses knowledge, so you may be filled with all the fullness of God.
—*Ephesians 3:17b–19*

Listen, my sons, to a father's discipline,
    and pay attention
    so that you may gain understanding,
for I am giving you good instruction.
    Don't abandon my teaching.
When I was a son with my father,
    tender and precious to my mother,
he taught me and said:
    "Your heart must hold on to my words.
    Keep my commands and live."
—*Proverbs 4:1–4*

For they are not meaningless words to you
but they are your life.
—*Deuteronomy 32:47a*

My son, if your heart is wise,
   my heart will indeed rejoice.
My innermost being will cheer
   when your lips say what is right.
Don't be jealous of sinners;
   instead, always fear the LORD.
For then you will have a future,
   and your hope will never fade.
   —*Proverbs 23:15–18*

Do you know a book you are willing to put under your head when you lay dying? That is the book you want to study while you are living. There is but one such Book in the world.
   —*Joseph Cook*

My son, pay attention to my words;
   listen closely to my sayings.
Don't lose sight of them;
   keep them within your heart.
For they are life to those who find them,
   and health to one's whole body.
Guard your heart above all else,
   for it is the source of life.
Don't let your mouth speak dishonestly,
   and don't let your lips talk deviously.
Let your eyes look forward;
   fix your gaze straight ahead.
Carefully consider the path for your feet,
   and all your ways will be established.
Don't turn to the right or to the left;
   keep your feet away from evil.
   —*Proverbs 4:20–27*

The Lord bless you and protect you;
    the Lord make His face shine on you,
    and be gracious to you;
the Lord look with favor on you
    and give you peace.
        —*Numbers 6:24–26*

May the Lord add to your numbers,
    both yours and your children's.
May you be blessed by the Lord,
    the Maker of heaven and earth.
        —*Psalm 115:14–15*

Go around Zion, encircle it;
    count its towers,
note its ramparts; tour its citadels
    so that you can tell a future generation:
"This God, our God forever and ever—
    He will lead us eternally."
        —*Psalm 48:12–14*

Your servants' children will dwell securely,
    and their offspring will be
    established before You.
        —*Psalm 102:28*

PROMISES
for
WHO YOU ARE

Some men are Christians in name only. Yet some of them still have a lot of nice stuff to show for it. Success has seemed to flow into their hands despite their fairly frequent disregard for God.

But others—like you—are deliberate believers, focused men of faith, men who love others well and pour importance into your roles and relationships.

So keep your eyes on God, who offers the truest sort of success through the path of faithfulness, obedience, and devotion. Your brand of life, sir, looks really good on you.

A MAN
of
WORTH

At Times, I Wonder How Much I Matter

The first man was from the earth
  and made of dust;
    the second man is from heaven.
Like the man made of dust,
    so are those who are made of dust;
like the heavenly man,
    so are those who are heavenly.
And just as we have borne
    the image of the man made of dust,
we will also bear the image
    of the heavenly man.
        —*1 Corinthians 15:47–49*

Do you not recognize for yourselves that Jesus Christ is in you?
—*Deuteronomy 13:5b*

For in Him we live and move and exist, as even some of your own poets have said, "For we are also His offspring."
—*Acts 17:28*

Therefore if anyone is in Christ, there is a new creation; old things have passed away, and look, new things have come.
—*2 Corinthians 5:17*

You took off your former way of life, the old man that is corrupted by deceitful desires; you are being renewed in the spirit of your minds; you put on the new man, the one created according to God's likeness in righteousness and purity of the truth.
—*Ephesians 4:22–24*

Brothers, consider your calling: not many are wise from a human perspective, not many powerful, not many of noble birth.

Instead, God has chosen the world's foolish things to shame the wise, and God has chosen the world's weak things to shame the strong.

God has chosen the world's insignificant and despised things—the things viewed as nothing—so He might bring to nothing the things that are viewed as something, so that no one can boast in His presence.

But from Him you are in Christ Jesus, who for us became wisdom from God, as well as righteousness, sanctification, and redemption, in order that, as it is written: "The one who boasts must boast in the Lord."
　—1 Corinthians 1:26–31

Indeed, it was for my own welfare
　　that I had such great bitterness;
but Your love has delivered me
　　from the Pit of destruction,
for You have thrown all my sins
　　behind Your back.
　　　—Isaiah 38:17

Who is a God like You,
    removing iniquity
and passing over rebellion
    for the remnant of His inheritance?
He does not hold on to His anger forever,
    because He delights in faithful love.
He will again have compassion on us;
    He will vanquish our iniquities.
You will cast all our sins
    into the depths of the sea.
        —*Micah 7:18–19*

He made the One who did not know sin
to be sin for us, so that we might become the
righteousness of God in Him.
        —*2 Corinthians 5:21*

All that I am, I owe to Jesus Christ,
revealed to me in his divine Book, the Bible.
        —*David Livingstone*

When I observe Your heavens,
    the work of Your fingers,
the moon and the stars,
    which You set in place,
what is man that You remember him,
    the son of man that You look after him?
You made him little less than God
    and crowned him with glory and honor.
You made him lord
    over the works of Your hands;
You put everything under his feet:
    all the sheep and oxen,
as well as animals in the wild,
    birds of the sky, and fish of the sea
    passing through the currents of the seas.
LORD, our Lord,
    how magnificent is Your name
    throughout the earth!
        —Psalm 8:3–9

He has not dealt with us as our sins deserve
    or repaid us according to our offenses.
For as high as the heavens are above the earth,
    so great is His faithful love
    toward those who fear Him.
As far as the east is from the west,
    so far has He removed
    our transgressions from us.
    —*Psalm 103:10–12*

How happy those whose lawless acts are
forgiven and whose sins are covered!
    —*Romans 4:7*

Therefore, brothers, since we have boldness
to enter the sanctuary through the blood of
Jesus, by the new and living way that He has
inaugurated for us, through the curtain (that is,
His flesh); and since we have a great high priest
over the house of God, let us draw near with a
true heart in full assurance of faith, our hearts
sprinkled clean from an evil conscience and
our bodies washed in pure water.
    —*Hebrews 10:19–22*

A MAN
of
INTEGRITY

Help Me Be the Person I Really Want to Be

I will pay attention to the way of integrity.
    When will You come to me?
I will live with integrity of heart in my house.
    I will not set anything
    godless before my eyes.
I hate the doing of transgression;
    it will not cling to me.
A devious heart will be far from me;
    I will not be involved with evil.
        —Psalm 101:2–4

A man who does not control his temper
　　is like a city whose wall is broken down.
　　　　—*Proverbs 25:28*

A fool gives full vent to his anger,
　　but a wise man holds it in check.
　　　　—*Proverbs 29:11*

A gossip goes around revealing a secret,
　　but the trustworthy keeps a confidence.
　　　　—*Proverbs 11:13*

For we are His creation—created in Christ
Jesus for good works, which God prepared
ahead of time so that we should walk in them.
　　　　—*Ephesians 2:10*

Righteousness guards people of integrity,
　　but wickedness undermines the sinner.
　　　　—*Proverbs 13:6*

Dear friends, if our hearts do not condemn us we have confidence before God, and can receive whatever we ask from Him because we keep His commands and do what is pleasing in His sight.

—*1 John 3:21–22*

For this is what love for God is: to keep His commands. Now His commands are not a burden.

—*1 John 5:3*

For this is God's will, your sanctification: that you abstain from sexual immorality, so that each of you knows how to possess his own vessel in sanctification and honor, not with lustful desires, like the Gentiles who don't know God.

This means one must not transgress against and defraud his brother in this matter, because the Lord is an avenger of all these offenses, as we also previously told and warned you. For God has not called us to impurity, but to sanctification.

—*1 Thessalonians 4:3–7*

For the one who wants to love life
    and to see good days
must keep his tongue from evil
    and his lips from speaking deceit,
and he must turn away from evil
    and do good.
He must seek peace and pursue it,
    because the eyes of the Lord
are on the righteous
    and His ears are open to their request.
        —*1 Peter 3:10–12a*

When you have read the Bible, you will
know it is the Word of God, because you will
have found it the key to your own heart, your
own happiness, and your own duty.
        —*Woodrow Wilson*

Now in a large house there are not only gold and silver bowls, but also those of wood and earthenware, some for special use, some for ordinary. So if anyone purifies himself from these things, he will be a special instrument, set apart, useful to the Master, prepared for every good work.

Flee from youthful passions, and pursue righteousness, faith, love, and peace, along with those who call on the Lord from a pure heart. But reject foolish and ignorant disputes, knowing that they breed quarrels.

The Lord's slave must not quarrel, but must be gentle to everyone, able to teach, and patient, instructing his opponents with gentleness. Perhaps God will grant them repentance to know the truth.

—*2 Timothy 2:20–25*

Walk as children of light—for the fruit of the light results in all goodness, righteousness, and truth—discerning what is pleasing to the Lord. Don't participate in the fruitless works of darkness, but instead, expose them. For it is shameful even to mention what is done by them in secret. Everything exposed by the light is made clear, for what makes everything clear is light.

—Ephesians 5:8b–14a

Therefore, God's chosen ones, holy and loved, put on heartfelt compassion, kindness, humility, gentleness, and patience, accepting one another and forgiving one another if anyone has a complaint against another. Just as the Lord has forgiven you, so also you must forgive. Above all, put on love—the perfect bond of unity.

—Colossians 3:12–14

Be alert, stand firm in the faith, be brave and strong. Your every action must be done with love.

—1 Corinthians 16:13–14

A MAN
on a
MISSION

This Is What I Was Put on This Earth to Do

If I walk in the thick of danger,
    You will preserve my life
    from the anger of my enemies.
You will extend Your hand;
    Your right hand will save me.
The LORD will fulfill His purpose for me.
    LORD, Your love is eternal;
    do not abandon the work of Your hands.
        —Psalm 138:7–8

Make your own attitude that of Christ Jesus,
    who, existing in the form of God,
did not consider equality with God
    as something to be used
    for His own advantage.
Instead He emptied Himself
    by assuming the form of a slave,
    taking on the likeness of men.
And when He had come
    as a man in His external form,
He humbled Himself by becoming obedient
    to the point of death—
    even to death on a cross.
For this reason God also highly exalted Him
    and gave Him the name
    that is above every name,
so that at the name of Jesus
    every knee should bow—
of those who are in heaven and on earth
    and under the earth—
and every tongue should confess
    that Jesus Christ is Lord,
    to the glory of God the Father.
        —Philippians 2:5–11

For me, living is Christ.
        —Philippians 1:21a

Dear friends, when the fiery ordeal arises among you to test you, don't be surprised by it, as if something unusual were happening to you.

Instead, as you share in the sufferings of the Messiah rejoice, so that you may also rejoice with great joy at the revelation of His glory.

If you are ridiculed for the name of Christ, you are blessed, because the Spirit of glory and of God rests on you.

—*1 Peter 4:12–14*

In fact, all those who want to live a godly life in Christ Jesus will be persecuted.

—*2 Timothy 3:12*

So don't be ashamed of the testimony about our Lord. . . . Instead, share in suffering for the gospel, relying on the power of God, who has saved us and called us with a holy calling, not according to our works, but according to His own purpose and grace, which was given to us in Christ Jesus before time began.

—*2 Timothy 1:8–9*

We know that all things work together for the good of those who love God: those who are called according to His purpose.
—*Romans 8:28*

Many plans are in a man's heart,
    but the LORD's decree will prevail.
—*Proverbs 19:21*

The Bible is to us what the star was to the wise men. But if we spend all our time in gazing upon it, observing its motions, and admiring its splendor without being led to Christ by it, the use of it will be lost to us.
—*Thomas Adams*

Get wisdom, get understanding;
 don't forget or turn away
 from the words of my mouth.
Don't abandon wisdom,
 and she will watch over you;
 love her, and she will guard you.
Wisdom is supreme—so get wisdom.
 And whatever else you get,
 get understanding.
Cherish her, and she will exalt you;
 if you embrace her, she will honor you.
She will place a garland of grace on your head;
 she will give you a crown of beauty. . . .
When you walk,
 your steps will not be hindered;
when you run,
 you will not stumble.
 —Proverbs 4:5–9, 12

For this reason also, since the day we heard this, we haven't stopped praying for you. We are asking that you may be filled with the knowledge of His will in all wisdom and spiritual understanding, so that you may walk worthy of the Lord, fully pleasing to Him, bearing fruit in every good work and growing in the knowledge of God.

May you be strengthened with all power, according to His glorious might, for all endurance and patience, with joy giving thanks to the Father, who has enabled you to share in the saints' inheritance in the light.

—*Colossians 1:9–12*

And in view of this, we always pray for you that our God will consider you worthy of His calling, and will, by His power, fulfill every desire for goodness and the work of faith, so that the name of our Lord Jesus will be glorified by you, and you by Him, according to the grace of our God and the Lord Jesus Christ.

—*2 Thessalonians 1:11–12*

A MAN
with a
PLAN

Lord, Show Me the Way You Want Me to Go

"For I know the plans I have for you"—
this is the LORD's declaration—"plans for your
welfare, not for disaster, to give you a future
and a hope. You will call to Me and come and
pray to Me, and I will listen to you. You will
seek Me and find Me when you search for Me
with all your heart."
—*Jeremiah 29:11–13*

Commit your activities to the LORD
    and your plans will be achieved.
        —Proverbs 16:3

Plans fail when there is no counsel,
    but with many advisers they succeed.
        —Proverbs 15:22

The counsel of the LORD stands forever,
    the plans of His heart
    from generation to generation.
        —Psalm 33:11

I know that You can do anything
    and no plan of Yours can be thwarted.
        —Job 42:2

May He give you what your heart desires
    and fulfill your whole purpose.
        —Psalm 20:4

What the wicked dreads will come to him,
    but what the righteous desires
    will be given to him.
        —*Proverbs 10:24*

Not that I have already reached the goal
or am already fully mature, but I make every
effort to take hold of it because I also have
been taken hold of by Christ Jesus.

Brothers, I do not consider myself to have
taken hold of it. But one thing I do: forgetting
what is behind and reaching forward to what
is ahead, I pursue as my goal the prize promised by God's heavenly call in Christ Jesus.
        —*Philippians 3:12–14*

For we know that if our earthly house,
a tent, is destroyed, we have a building from
God, a house not made with hands, eternal in
the heavens. . . . And the One who prepared
us for this very thing is God, who gave us the
Spirit as a down payment.
        —*2 Corinthians 5:1, 5*

Though we are always confident and know that while we are at home in the body we are away from the Lord—for we walk by faith, not by sight—yet we are confident and satisfied to be out of the body and at home with the Lord. Therefore, whether we are at home or away, we make it our aim to be pleasing to Him.
—*2 Corinthians 5:6–9*

For we are convinced that we have a clear conscience, wanting to conduct ourselves honorably in everything.
—*Hebrews 13:18b*

The Word of God will stand a thousand readings. And he who has gone over it most frequently is the surest of finding new wonders there.
—*James Hamilton*

Commit your way to the LORD;
　　trust in Him, and He will act,
making your righteousness shine like the dawn,
　　your justice like the noonday.
Be silent before the LORD
　　and wait expectantly for Him;
do not be agitated by one
　　who prospers in his way,
　　by the man who carries out evil plans.
Refrain from anger and give up your rage;
　　do not be agitated—it can only bring harm.
For evildoers will be destroyed,
　　but those who put their hope in the LORD
　　will inherit the land.
　　　—Psalm 37:5–9

The Lord brings poverty and gives wealth;
   He humbles and He exalts.
He raises the poor from the dust
   and lifts the needy from the garbage pile.
He seats them with noblemen
   and gives them a throne of honor.
For the foundations
   of the earth are the Lord's;
   He has set the world on them.
He guards the steps of His faithful ones,
   but the wicked are silenced in darkness,
for a man does not prevail
   by his own strength.
   —*1 Samuel 2:7–9*

   I am able to do all things through Him
who strengthens me.
   —*Philippians 4:13*

No wisdom, no understanding, and no counsel
   will prevail against the Lord.
A horse is prepared for the day of battle,
   but victory comes from the Lord.
   —*Proverbs 21:30–31*

A MAN
of
HIS WORD

Give Me a New Hunger for the Bible

I will meditate on Your precepts
    and think about Your ways.
I will delight in Your statutes;
    I will not forget Your word. . . .
Your statutes are the theme of my song
    during my earthly life.
I remember Your name in the night, LORD,
    and I keep Your law.
This is my practice:
    I obey Your precepts.
        —*Psalm 119:15–16, 54–56*

Every word of God is pure;
    He is a shield to those
    who take refuge in Him.
        —*Proverbs 30:5*

How happy are those whose way is blameless,
    who live according to the law of the Lord!
Happy are those who keep His decrees
    and seek Him with all their heart.
        —*Psalm 119:1–2*

For whatever was written before was
written for our instruction, so that through
our endurance and through the encouragement
of the Scriptures we may have hope.
        —*Romans 15:4*

Remember Your word to Your servant;
    You have given me hope through it.
This is my comfort in my affliction:
    Your promise has given me life.
        —*Psalm 119:49–50*

As for you, continue in what you have learned and firmly believed, knowing those from whom you learned, and that from childhood you have known the sacred Scriptures, which are able to instruct you for salvation through faith in Christ Jesus.
—*2 Timothy 3:14–15*

The wise will be put to shame;
    they will be dismayed and snared.
They have rejected the word of the LORD,
    so what wisdom do they really have?
—*Jeremiah 8:9*

I have Your decrees as a heritage forever;
    indeed, they are the joy of my heart.
I am resolved to obey Your statutes
    to the very end.
—*Psalm 119:111–112*

Your word is completely pure,
    and Your servant loves it.
—*Psalm 119:140*

LORD, Your word is forever;
     it is firmly fixed in heaven. . . .
They stand today in accordance
     with Your judgments,
     for all things are Your servants.
If Your instruction had not been my delight,
     I would have died in my affliction.
I will never forget Your precepts,
     for You have given me life through them. . . .
I have seen a limit to all perfection,
     but Your command is without limit.
          —Psalm 119:89, 91–93, 96

God himself has condescended to teach the way. For this very end he came from heaven. And he hath written it down in a book. O give me that Book! At any price, give me the Book of God!
          —John Wesley

The instruction of the LORD is perfect,
    reviving the soul;
the testimony of the LORD is trustworthy,
    making the inexperienced wise.
The precepts of the LORD are right,
    making the heart glad;
the commandment of the LORD is radiant,
    making the eyes light up.
The fear of the LORD is pure,
    enduring forever;
the ordinances of the LORD are reliable
    and altogether righteous.
They are more desirable than gold—
    than an abundance of pure gold;
and sweeter than honey—
    than honey dripping from the comb.
In addition, Your servant is warned by them;
    there is great reward in keeping them.
        —*Psalm 19:7–11*

I delight to do Your will, my God;
    Your instruction resides within me.
        —Psalm 40:8

Your decrees are my delight
    and my counselors.
        —Psalm 119:24

I rejoice in the way revealed by Your decrees
    as much as in all riches.
        —Psalm 119:14

Long ago I learned from Your decrees
    that You have established them forever.
        —Psalm 119:152

The entirety of Your word is truth,
    and all Your righteous judgments
    endure forever.
        —Psalm 119:160

PROMISES
for a
LIVING
FAITH

Little things: Making sure you're in church on Sunday. Making sure the day doesn't start until you've met God in prayer. Making sure others have theirs before you get yours.

The Christian life began with a big thing: Jesus Christ coming to earth, dying on a cross to forgive our sins, returning to life to make death a toothless enemy. But the Christian life bears fruit in the little things—the little things people admire in you, the little you add to an ordinary day, the little things you do that make your life a blessing to so many.

A Heart
for
Worship

I'll Praise You Today, I'll Praise You Forever

Better a day in Your courts
    than a thousand anywhere else.
I would rather be at the door
    of the house of my God
    than to live in the tents of the wicked.
For the LORD God is a sun and shield.
    The LORD gives grace and glory;
He does not withhold the good
    from those who live with integrity.
        —*Psalm 84:10–11*

Come, let us worship and bow down;
    let us kneel before the LORD our Maker.
For He is our God,
    and we are the people of His pasture,
    the sheep under His care.
        —Psalm 95:6–7a

We all went astray like sheep;
    we all have turned to our own way;
and the LORD has punished Him
    for the iniquity of us all.
        —Isaiah 53:6

    For you know the grace of our Lord Jesus Christ: although He was rich, for your sake He became poor, so that by His poverty you might become rich.
        —2 Corinthians 8:9

My salvation and glory depend on God;
    my strong rock, my refuge, is in God.
Trust in Him at all times, you people;
    pour out your hearts before Him.
    God is our refuge.
        —Psalm 62:7–8

Whom do I have in heaven but You?
    And I desire nothing on earth but You.
My flesh and my heart may fail,
    but God is the strength of my heart,
    my portion forever.
        —*Psalm 73:25–26*

God—His way is perfect;
    the word of the LORD is pure.
He is a shield to all
    who take refuge in Him.
For who is God besides the LORD?
    And who is a rock? Only our God.
God—He clothes me with strength
    and makes my way perfect.
He makes my feet like the feet of a deer
    and sets me securely on the heights.
        —*Psalm 18:30–33*

Clap your hands, all you peoples;
    shout to God with a jubilant cry.
For the LORD Most High is awe-inspiring,
    a great King over all the earth.
        —*Psalm 47:1–2*

Shout triumphantly to the LORD,
   all the earth.
Serve the LORD with gladness;
   come before Him with joyful songs.
Acknowledge that the LORD is God.
   He made us, and we are His—
   His people, the sheep of His pasture.
Enter His gates with thanksgiving
   and His courts with praise.
Give thanks to Him and praise His name.
   For the LORD is good,
   and His love is eternal;
His faithfulness endures
   through all generations.
   —*Psalm 100:1–5*

   The Bible furnishes the only fitting vehicle
to express the thoughts that overwhelm us
when contemplating the stellar universe.
   —*O. M. Mitchell*

Ascribe to the LORD, families of the peoples,
   ascribe to the LORD glory and strength.
Ascribe to the LORD the glory of His name;
   bring an offering and come before Him.
Worship the LORD
   in the splendor of His holiness;
   tremble before Him, all the earth.
The world is firmly established;
   it cannot be shaken.
Let the heavens be glad and the earth rejoice,
   and let them say among the nations,
"The LORD is King!"
Let the sea and everything in it resound;
   let the fields and all that is in them exult.
Then the trees of the forest will shout for joy
before the LORD,
   for He is coming to judge the earth.
   —*1 Chronicles 16:28–33*

Oh, the depth of the riches
    both of the wisdom
    and the knowledge of God!
How unsearchable His judgments
    and untraceable His ways!
For who has known the mind of the Lord?
    Or who has been His counselor?
Or who has ever first given to Him,
    and has to be repaid?
For from Him and through Him
    and to Him are all things.
    To Him be the glory forever.
        —*Romans 11:33–36*

Let the message about the Messiah dwell
richly among you, teaching and admonishing
one another in all wisdom, and singing psalms,
hymns, and spiritual songs, with gratitude in
your hearts to God.
        —*Colossians 3:16*

May the LORD, the God of Israel, be praised
    from everlasting to everlasting.
        —*1 Chronicles 16:36*

A Hunger

for

Prayer

Underneath, I Am So Dependent upon You

Asa cried out to the LORD his God: "LORD, there is no one besides You to help the mighty and those without strength. Help us, LORD our God, for we depend on You, and in Your name we have come against this multitude. LORD, You are our God. Do not let a mere mortal hinder You."

—*2 Chronicles 14:11*

Let me experience
    Your faithful love in the morning,
    for I trust in You.
Reveal to me the way I should go,
    because I long for You.
Rescue me from my enemies, LORD;
    I come to You for protection.
Teach me to do Your will,
    for You are my God.
May Your gracious Spirit
    lead me on level ground.
        —Psalm 143:8–10

Now this is the confidence we have before Him: whenever we ask anything according to His will, He hears us. And if we know that He hears whatever we ask, we know that we have what we have asked Him for.
        —1 John 5:14–15

Keep asking, and it will be given to you. Keep searching, and you will find. Keep knocking, and the door will be opened to you.
        —Matthew 7:7

I cry aloud to God,
    aloud to God, and He will hear me.
        —*Psalm 77:1*

The LORD is near all who call out to Him,
    all who call out to Him with integrity.
He fulfills the desires of those who fear Him;
    He hears their cry for help and saves them.
        —*Psalm 145:18–19*

You will pray to Him,
    and He will hear you . . .
    and light will shine on your ways
        —*Job 22:27a, 28b*

Be gracious to me, Lord,
    for I call to You all day long.
Bring joy to Your servant's life,
    since I set my hope on You, Lord.
For You, Lord, are kind and ready to forgive,
    abundant in faithful love
    to all who call on You.
        —*Psalm 86:3–5*

God, You are my God;
  I eagerly seek You.
I thirst for You; my body faints for You
  in a land that is dry,
  desolate, and without water.
So I gaze on You in the sanctuary
  to see Your strength and Your glory.
My lips will glorify You
  because Your faithful love
  is better than life.
So I will praise You as long as I live;
  at Your name, I will lift up my hands.
You satisfy me as with rich food;
  my mouth will praise You with joyful lips.
  —*Psalm 63:1–5*

I know the Bible is inspired because it finds
me at greater depths of my being than any
other book.
  —*Samuel Taylor Coleridge*

Come and see the works of God;
    His acts toward mankind
    are awe-inspiring.
Come and listen, all who fear God,
    and I will tell what He has done for me.
I cried out to Him with my mouth,
    and praise was on my tongue.
If I had been aware of malice in my heart,
    the Lord would not have listened.
However, God has listened;
    He has paid attention
    to the sound of my prayer.
May God be praised!
    He has not turned away my prayer
    or turned His faithful love from me.
    —*Psalm 66:5, 16–20*

Call on Me in a day of trouble;
　　I will rescue you, and you will honor Me.
　　　　—Psalm 50:15

Even before they call, I will answer;
　　while they are still speaking, I will hear.
　　　　—Isaiah 65:24

How happy is the man
　　who has put his trust in the LORD
and has not turned to the proud
　　or to those who run after lies!
LORD my God,
　　You have done many things—
Your wonderful works and Your plans for us;
　　none can compare with You.
If I were to report and speak of them,
　　they are more than can be told.
　　　　—Psalm 40:4–5

But as for me, I will look to the LORD;
　　I will wait for the God of my salvation.
　　My God will hear me.
　　　　—Micah 7:7

A BURDEN
for
OTHERS

Being Selfish Is So Easy, and So Unsatisfying

Now finally, all of you should be like-minded and sympathetic, should love believers, and be compassionate and humble, not paying back evil for evil or insult for insult but, on the contrary, giving a blessing, since you were called for this, so that you can inherit a blessing.
—*1 Peter 3:8–9*

"Everything is permissible," but not everything builds up. No one should seek his own good, but the good of the other person.
—*1 Corinthians 10:23b–24*

If a brother or sister is without clothes and lacks daily food, and one of you says to them, "Go in peace, keep warm, and eat well," but you don't give them what the body needs, what good is it?
—*James 2:15–16*

But when you give to the poor, don't let your left hand know what your right hand is doing, so that your giving may be in secret. And your Father who sees in secret will reward you.
—*Matthew 6:3–4*

Therefore, through Him let us continually offer up to God a sacrifice of praise, that is, the fruit of our lips that confess His name. Don't neglect to do good and to share, for God is pleased with such sacrifices.
—*Hebrews 13:15–16*

Render true justice. Show faithful love and compassion to one another. Do not oppress the widow or the fatherless, the stranger or the poor, and do not plot evil in your hearts against one another.

—Zechariah 7:9b–10

All bitterness, anger and wrath, insult and slander must be removed from you, along with all wickedness. And be kind and compassionate to one another, forgiving one another, just as God also forgave you in Christ.

—Ephesians 4:31–32

Carry one another's burdens; in this way you will fulfill the law of Christ.

—Galatians 6:2

For where envy and selfish ambition exist, there is disorder and every kind of evil. But the wisdom from above is first pure, then peace-loving, gentle, compliant, full of mercy and good fruits, without favoritism and hypocrisy.

—James 3:16–17

The one who despises his neighbor sins,
    but whoever shows kindness
    to the poor will be happy.
       —Proverbs 14:21

The one who oppresses the poor
    insults their Maker,
but one who is kind
    to the needy honors Him.
       —Proverbs 14:31

A generous person will be enriched,
    and the one who gives a drink of water
    will receive water.
       —Proverbs 11:25

I read my Bible to know what people ought to be doing, and my newspaper to know what they are doing.
       —John Henry Newman

Isn't the fast I choose:
    To break the chains of wickedness,
to untie the ropes of the yoke,
    to set the oppressed free,
    and to tear off every yoke?
Is it not to share your bread with the hungry,
    to bring the poor and homeless
    into your house,
to clothe the naked when you see him,
    and to not ignore
    your own flesh and blood?
Then your light will appear like the dawn,
    and your recovery will come quickly.
Your righteousness will go before you,
    and the LORD's glory
    will be your rear guard.
At that time, when you call,
    the LORD will answer;
when you cry out,
    He will say: Here I am.
        —*Isaiah 58:6–9*

Do nothing out of rivalry or conceit, but in humility consider others as more important than yourselves. Everyone should look out not only for his own interests, but also for the interests of others.

—*Philippians 2:3–4*

Since you put away lying, speak the truth, each one to his neighbor, because we are members of one another.

No rotten talk should come from your mouth, but only what is good for the building up of someone in need, in order to give grace to those who hear.

—*Ephesians 4:25, 29*

Now may the God of peace, who brought up from the dead our Lord Jesus—the great Shepherd of the sheep—with the blood of the everlasting covenant, equip you with all that is good to do His will, working in us what is pleasing in His sight, through Jesus Christ, to whom be glory forever and ever.

—*Hebrews 13:20–21*

A NEED
for
ACCOUNT-
ABILITY

Whatever I Need to Do to Stay True

I pray that your participation in the faith may become effective through knowing every good thing that is in us for the glory of Christ.

For I have great joy and encouragement from your love, because the hearts of the saints have been refreshed through you, brother.

—Philemon 6–7

How good and pleasant it is
    when brothers can live together! . . .
For there the LORD
    has appointed the blessing—
    life forevermore.
        —*Psalm 133:1, 3b*

Therefore, brothers, stand firm and hold to the traditions you were taught, either by our message or by our letter. May our Lord Jesus Christ Himself and God our Father, who has loved us and given us eternal encouragement and good hope by grace, encourage your hearts and strengthen you in every good work and word.
        —*2 Thessalonians 2:15–17*

Let us hold on to the confession of our hope without wavering, for He who promised is faithful. And let us be concerned about one another in order to promote love and good works, not staying away from our meetings, as some habitually do, but encouraging each other, and all the more as you see the day drawing near.
        —*Hebrews 10:23–25*

A friend loves at all times,
    and a brother is born for a difficult time.
        —*Proverbs 17:17*

A man with many friends may be harmed,
    but there is a friend
    who stays closer than a brother.
        —*Proverbs 18:24*

I am a friend to all who fear You,
    to those who keep Your precepts.
        —*Psalm 119:63*

The wounds of a friend are trustworthy.
        —*Proverbs 27:6a*

It is better to listen to rebuke
    from a wise person
    than to listen to the song of fools.
        —*Ecclesiastes 7:5*

Teach me, and I will be silent.
    Help me understand what I did wrong.
        —*Job 6:24*

The one who says he is in the light but hates his brother is in the darkness until now. The one who loves his brother remains in the light, and there is no cause for stumbling in him.

—*1 John 2:9–10*

Anyone who ignores instruction
despises himself,
but whoever listens to correction
acquires good sense.
—*Proverbs 15:32*

We read the Bible to be fed. We read it to be converted, to be strengthened, to be taught, to be rebuked, to be counseled, to be comforted.

—*Richard Foster*

How happy is the man
   who does not follow
   the advice of the wicked,
or take the path of sinners,
   or join a group of mockers!
Instead, his delight is in the LORD's instruction,
   and he meditates on it day and night.
He is like a tree
   planted beside streams of water
   that bears its fruit in season
and whose leaf does not wither.
   Whatever he does prospers. . . .
For the LORD watches over
   the way of the righteous,
   but the way of the wicked leads to ruin.
   —*Psalm 1:1–3, 6*

Watch out, brothers, so that there won't be in any of you an evil, unbelieving heart that departs from the living God. But encourage each other daily, while it is still called today, so that none of you is hardened by sin's deception.

For we have become companions of the Messiah if we hold firmly until the end the reality that we had at the start.

—*Hebrews 3:12–14*

Love must be without hypocrisy. Detest evil; cling to what is good. Show family affection to one another with brotherly love. Outdo one another in showing honor.

—*Romans 12:9–10*

Now may the God of endurance and encouragement grant you agreement with one another, according to Christ Jesus, so that you may glorify the God and Father of our Lord Jesus Christ with a united mind and voice. Therefore accept one another, just as the Messiah also accepted you, to the glory of God.

—*Romans 15:5–7*

A PASSION
for
LIVING

Life with God Is the Only Life I Want

Blessed be the God and Father of our Lord Jesus Christ. According to His great mercy, He has given us a new birth into a living hope through the resurrection of Jesus Christ from the dead, and into an inheritance that is imperishable, uncorrupted, and unfading, kept in heaven for you, who are being protected by God's power through faith for a salvation that is ready to be revealed in the last time.
—*1 Peter 1:3–5*

Dear friends, we are God's children now,
and what we will be has not yet been revealed.
We know that when He appears, we will be
like Him, because we will see Him as He is.
And everyone who has this hope in Him
purifies himself just as He is pure.
—*1 John 3:2–3*

The hope of the righteous is joy,
    but the expectation of the wicked
    comes to nothing.
        —*Proverbs 10:28*

I keep the LORD in mind always.
    Because He is at my right hand,
    I will not be shaken.
Therefore my heart is glad,
    and my spirit rejoices;
    my body also rests securely.
For You will not abandon me to Sheol;
    You will not allow Your Faithful One
    to see the Pit.
You reveal the path of life to me;
    in Your presence is abundant joy;
    in Your right hand are eternal pleasures.
        —*Psalm 16:8–11*

If we have placed our hope in Christ for this life only, we should be pitied more than anyone.
—*1 Corinthians 15:13*

For we too were once foolish, disobedient, deceived, captives of various passions and pleasures, living in malice and envy, hateful, detesting one another. But when the goodness and love for man appeared from God our Savior, He saved us—not by works of righteousness that we had done, but according to His mercy, through the washing of regeneration and renewal by the Holy Spirit.
—*Titus 3:3–5*

For when you were slaves of sin, you were free from allegiance to righteousness. And what fruit was produced then from the things you are now ashamed of? For the end of those things is death.

But now, since you have been liberated from sin and become enslaved to God, you have your fruit, which results in sanctification—and the end is eternal life!
—*Romans 6:20–22*

We have obtained access by faith into this grace in which we stand, and we rejoice in the hope of the glory of God. And not only that, but we also rejoice in our afflictions, because we know that affliction produces endurance, endurance produces proven character, and proven character produces hope.

This hope does not disappoint, because God's love has been poured out in our hearts through the Holy Spirit who was given to us.
—*Romans 5:2b–5*

The Bible is the truest utterance that ever came by alphabetic letters, through which, as through a window divinely opened, all men can look into the stillness of eternity and discern in glimpses their far-distant, long-forgotten home.
—*Thomas Carlyle*

Listen! I am telling you a mystery:
    We will not all fall asleep,
but we will all be changed,
    in a moment,
in the twinkling of an eye,
    at the last trumpet. . . .
Now when this corruptible
    is clothed with incorruptibility,
        and this mortal is clothed with immortality,
then the saying that is written will take place:
    Death has been swallowed up in victory.
O Death, where is your victory?
    O Death, where is your sting?
Now the sting of death is sin,
    and the power of sin is the law.
But thanks be to God, who gives us the victory
    through our Lord Jesus Christ!
        —*1 Corinthians 15:51–52a, 54–57*

So if you have been raised with the Messiah, seek what is above, where the Messiah is, seated at the right hand of God. Set your minds on what is above, not on what is on the earth.

For you have died, and your life is hidden with the Messiah in God. When the Messiah, who is your life, is revealed, then you also will be revealed with Him in glory.

—*Colossians 3:1–4*

For the grace of God has appeared, with salvation for all people, instructing us to deny godlessness and worldly lusts and to live in a sensible, righteous, and godly way in the present age, while we wait for the blessed hope and the appearing of the glory of our great God and Savior, Jesus Christ.

—*Titus 2:11–13*

Now may the God of hope fill you with all joy and peace in believing, so that you may overflow with hope by the power of the Holy Spirit.

—*Romans 15:13*